The Gift of Not Finding

Poems for Meditation

The Gift of Not Finding

Poems for Meditation

Carol Alena Aronoff, PhD

Homestead Lighthouse Press
Grants Pass, Oregon

The Gift of Not Finding: Poems for Meditation Copyright © 2020 by Carol Alena Aronoff. All rights reserved. No part of this book may be reproduced or transmitted in any form without the prior written permission of the publisher.

ISBN 978-1-950475-05-6
Library of Congress Control Number:

Homestead Lighthouse Press
1668 NE Foothill Boulevard
Unit A
Grants Pass, OR 97526
www.homesteadlighthousepress.com

Distributed by Homestead Lighthouse Press, Amazon.com, Barnes & Noble

Homestead Lighthouse Press gratefully acknowledges the generous support of its readers and patrons.

Book design by Ray Rhamey

For the spiritual teachers I've had the privilege to meet, for the love and support of friends and family, fellow poets and travelers, thank you! I am especially grateful to Donna McLaughlin for her wisdom, kindness and selfless support.

May we all awaken for the benefit of everyone.

Acknowledgments

I would like to thank the editors of the following publications for including some of my poems, sometimes in slightly different form:

Bosque, "Taos Summer"

Zingara Poetry, "Softly" (accepted as poetry pick)

Shattered Anthology, "Descent"

The Ghazal Page, "Dreaming Women in Rain"

Elementary My Dear Anthology, "Blood of the Soil"

Origami, "Make Offerings"

Tranquility Anthology, "The Nature of Prayer," 'The Gift of Quietude," 'A Geography of Stillness'

Sourland Review, "On Losing One's Head," "Meditation Through the Night"

Jete Away Anthology, "Freedom," "Dancing in the Heart of the Void"

Jellyfish Whispers, "Flow," "A Place for Hummingbirds," "Nesting

Dove Tales, Empathy in Art: Embracing the Other, "Make Offerings," "Tapestry of Undivided Wholeness"

Without Words Anthology, "Unnamed," "Breathing into Stillness, ""Presence"

Panoplyzine, "Mapless "

Wilda Morris's December Poetry Challenge, "The Turn"

Nature/Writing, "Nesting," "White Birds," Sparrow Encounter"

Amethyst Review, "The Blessing of Rain," "Prayer Flags"

Young Ravens Literary Review, "The Taste of Gratitude," "Now You See It . . ."

The Beautiful Space- A Journal of Mind, Art and Poetry, "Wisdom Blooms"

Minute magazine, "Illusion's Beauty"

Otherwise Engaged Journal, "Infinity of Death"

Total Eclipse, "Noticing," "Unreflected," "The Sound of the Moon"

Verse of Silence; You Can Hear the Ocean: An Anthology of Classic and Current Poetry, "The Muse"

Foreword

The Gift of Not Finding: Poems for Meditation by Carol Alena Aronoff embodies stillness.
Perhaps this is the secret goal of all poetry when it is most fit in consciousness and memory. For what does one desire more than peace and the absence of worry and speculation it brings? Poetry that achieves and evokes stillness—dare I say 'perfect' stillness—is a gift that allows one to breathe deeply and *be* love.

    The stillness and universal awareness evoked by these poems offer readers a safe yet thrilling space for grounding in the sweet loam of poetry. Doesn't exceptional poetry make us feel like the plants and trees we really are? In the perfect stillness of a poem one experiences this: anything is possible. This must be especially true for poems conceived as guides, prompts or companions for meditation.

    There are other qualities at work in this exquisite volume.

    Dreaming Women in Rain, a Ghazal for Agha Shahid Ali is so graceful. It makes heart-sense and a sound like a beautiful bell. The typographic playfulness in the poem *Let Be* deftly mirrors the playfulness of spirit, the wisdom, the light spiritual touch, the grace that is both Carol Aronoff *and* her poetry.

    "Desire is the Siren beckoning/just out of reach." In one line, this is the essence of Aronoff's poetry. Her poems are seductive. They wrap one up in gauzy, shimmering layers through which the reader perceives openings to otherwise invisible places, places so desirable one aches to enter, touch and experience them. Yet, wisely, there is also in the experience the essence of the unattainable—so close, so ephemeral. Only the finest mystical poetry can accomplish such soul travel and sensuality.

As she asks later in another poem, *Dance Steps to the Edge of the Void*, "What is the difference/between wanting and not wanting?" That place—*the difference between*—is where poets and poetry keep house. It is where this poet, especially, thrives.

Aronoff's poems look under the leaves. They embody the particles that make up the beams of moonlight. Her poems delve beneath rocks, deep into the soil and mingle with the bones of our ancestors. We are *nada*, we murmur in the silence. We and the world are One. The best poetry takes us there and reaffirms this great truth. These poems embody the gift of the essence of meditation, the gift that everyone so urgently needs now.

Robert McDowell

Contents

Acknowledgments	i
Foreword	iii
Contents	v
The Gift of Not Finding	ix
Section I. Unimpeded Sky	1
A Taste of One Taste	2
Inseparable	4
White Birds	5
Remembrance	6
Flight of Fancy	7
The Nature of Duality	8
The Unraveling Heart	9
Just As They Are	10
A Generous Lover	12
The Nature of Prayer	13
The Blessing of Rain	15
A Place for Hummingbirds	16
Presence	18
A Hint of Peace	20
Dance Steps to the Edge of the Void	22
Flow	23
In Search of the Changeless Heart	24
Dreaming Women in Rain	25
Softly	27
Noticing	28
A Glimpse of Awakening	29

Infinity of Death	30
Changeless Awareness	31
Freedom	32
Hozho	33
Make Offerings	35
Section II. The Laughter of Stones	39
Blood of the Soil	40
Waking Up	41
Taos Summer	42
Traveling Light	43
The Door	44
Descent	45
Stoned	47
The Dalai Lama Speaks of Peace at the Maui War Memorial	48
Now You See It . . .	50
Always There	51
A Simple Task	52
A Lover's Prayer	53
The Gift of Quietude	54
Nothing to Do	55
A Question of Love	56
Illusion's Beauty	57
On Losing One's Head	59
Sparrow Encounter	60
Weather Report	61
Some Day	62
No Need to Explain	63
Mapless	65
Inspiration	66
Uncovered	67
Nesting	69

The Gift of Not Finding

The Muse	70
The Taste of Gratitude	71
Meditation Through the Night	72
Section III. Geography of Stillness	75
At the Beginning	76
Grounding	77
Space	78
Meditation on Watching Thoughts	79
A Geography of Stillness	81
The Fullness of Emptiness	82
Breathing into Stillness	83
Being	85
New Year's Resolution	86
Letting Go	88
Tapestry of Undivided Wholeness	89
One Question	90
Wisdom Blooms	91
What Remains	92
What if	93
Not the Way You Think	94
Prayer flags	95
The Turn	96
As Earth's Rotation Slows	97
Ode to the Emptiness of Moon	98
Unnamed	99
Essential Nature	100
The Gift Of ( )	102
Who knows	103
Let Be	104
Dancing in the Heart of the Void	106
About the Author	107

The Gift of Not Finding

Place your mind softly
as silk curtains
in the stillness of space.
Let mind's whisper
fade like sunset,
subtle traces
intimate with sky.

Rest in awareness—
all-inclusive, luminous
presence, invariably
filling, forming, emptying—
changeless as mirror,
ephemeral home
to passersby.

Stillness undisturbed
by movement. Experiencer
just another experience.
Where is the one
who knows this?
Where is the one
who cannot be found?

Section I
Unimpeded Sky

A Taste of One Taste

If you love the thorn,
the pricked finger,
the one who has
been pricked,
if you forget
what was
so important
a minute ago
but relish
the moment,
if you include
the world,
this wild,
unexpected
tapestry:
woven strands
of form and color
without here or there,
mine or yours-
you will find
at its core:
openness
and bliss.
Not the silence
that excludes
all sound,
nor the happiness

confined to lovers,
not the peace
squeezed out of
conflict's absence,
but a full-throated
hurrah-
the joyful
communion
with everything.

Inseparable

To watch a raindrop slide
off stone and hear the curl
of nectar on hummingbird
tongue slows time to dazzling.
The world opens-morning
glory unfolding, swift wings
dipping, then lifting into wind.
Palm fronds sway, thoughts
swirl, yet you can taste
the stillness-no different from
the dance of warp and weft,
the rise and fall of breath
with no one breathing.

White Birds

Sky has no past.
It doesn't recall the clouds
from yesterday nor stars
winking out this morning.

A flock of small birds circles
above the road, wings flickering
white gold against azure
as they turn, one body.

Do they know I am watching?
When I return,
will they still be there?
Will I?

Remembrance

It is good to remember
that moonflowers bloom
only at night,
that trillium needs
seven years
to grow from seed
to flower.

Some things take
longer to ripen,
others last
only a moment
before fading
beyond memory.
Like life.

Flight of Fancy

A cloud train brushes the crest
of a nearby mountain as it rolls
toward the sea; it mutes
the sequins and tinfoil sunset
draped over sky at horizon's edge.
Watching this collage in motion,
I yearn to join the parade, to lift
on hawk wing, float on subtle
currents and land where I may.
No plans, no ideas about where
or how I ought to be. No thoughts
at all. Just feather light awareness

      drifting

              on

                      a fledgling breeze.

The Nature of Duality

Sky's sorrow brings gladioli to their peak,
small compensation for a sadness of stars
dimmed by full moon. One thing offsets
another: rouged clouds beneath lapis lazuli
roof, wavering sea against certain shore.
Who knows what hangs in the balance,
what metaphors float on poetic currents
or sail to far horizons on wings of steel?
Opposites will always find their tensile
strength before transcendence. The two
reveal their source as one.

The Unraveling Heart

Sometimes it's like this:
the door partly open,
Mynahs in the mango tree
chattering as if no one
can hear. The heart's web
of if onlys swept away
by the splendor of nature.
No conditions, no regrets
lingering.

Breathing in ocean,
the heart unravels.
No judgments to ripple
waves, the perceiver takes
in everything. A leaf floats,
sweeps the sand kissing
shadows. Open to life,
the heart remembers.

Love is like this.

Just As They Are

Clouds perch above the ocean
as sentinels and clowns. Day doesn't
mind. Sun will climb its usual path
undaunted by droplets and sky will
still be clear beyond its veil.

What some call partly cloudy
or scattered showers, mind knows
are passing thoughts. What if we saw
that same bright sky no matter
the outlook?

We could just ignore the forecasts.
We don't believe them anyway.
Headlines love to hook us into
wanting more. We are mice in the attic
of old news and yellowed paper.

If mindful of the dream we think
is real, loss and gain will trickle
through our fingers without getting
caught on spider webs. Even
geckoes will applaud us.

In the shadow of rainbow shower tree,
nameless fears will settle to the ground
if left alone, nonchalant blossoms

stirred only by breeze. No need to call
them back to feel more solid.

We can choose to allow all-comers,
sounds of suffering and joy, cicadas
and centipedes, just as they are. Not
weather, ephemeral, nor elements' subtle
changes will matter to this unimpeded sky.

A Generous Lover

A blush returns to sky's cheeks.
Morning. The drear of pewter
and faded denim lightens. Because
sun wakes, clouds of flamingo
feathers, the day promising.

Because there are two, the heart
unfurls. Call it love. The sound
of laughter. Hope slipping
through leaf-shaded branches,
sipping nectar with honeycreepers.

Because there is tenderness, nothing
missing. Beauty. Sorrow.
Separation's scar. The flowering
of grief and unending bliss.
Afternoon, a generous lover.

The Nature of Prayer

A rosary of flowers,
a litany of birdsong,
cricketspeak and
traveler's palm
percussion.
No need to light
candles as sun
illuminates the space
between branches
and leaves, warms
the petals of plumeria
and puakenekene
so they release their
fine incense to fill
the air with scents
of the sacred.

Nature's temples,
uncontrived,
abide in silence
and beauty,
surrounded by
swirl and torrent-
cycles of tumult
and calm inseparable.
All part of that divine,
seamless fabric

imbued with
intelligence and spirit,
patterned and naked
awareness. No need
to pray or ask for
anything, just rest.

The Blessing of Rain

The meadow folds in on itself
with an approaching squall.
Tall grasses lean over,
form shelters for mongeese
and other small creatures:
a casual benevolence
mothers know.

The air sizzles, sky larks wing
back to nests and hatchlings.
Kukui leaves tremble, turn upward
showing silvery slips. A lone
frog takes cover beneath
a banana leaf. Does it need
anything? Or think of death?

Prelude to the deluge, wind
drives clouds across grim sky,
then bows in silence at Gaia's
altar. The momentary hush
is filled with holiness, everything
just as it is. Rain's benediction
descends as truth, the elixir
of unspoken mystery.

A Place for Hummingbirds

A clutch of hummingbird eggs nestled
in seed down and feathers, bound
together with spider silk mixed
with paint chips and flowers-rests
in the pocket of an apron hanging
on a clothesline. Safe from predators.

A light bulb in the basement, beneath
a bridge, in a culvert or deep ravine.
In the unremembered. The thin shell
between us where we hide what's
most precious. Where we break.

Out of sight, in that cradle of silence,
the cocooning of seedlings and small
things. A fluttering, giving vent to,
birthing its opposite to see itself.
Those moments, when forgetting

is an art form, spectacular sunrise free
of restraint, we revel in the absence
of veils and artifice, all separation-
recognize the call of bird wings
to a more authentic place to rest.
An aerie open on all sides with no

ground. Nameless. No maps or

The Gift of Not Finding

hidden corners, seamless flow
of river and rain. We cannot remain
there too long, just long enough
for understanding to dawn. Like
hummingbirds, we seek refuge

Presence

Lost in thought- labyrinths of poppies
and circumstance, memory whorls
and run-on sentences- it is easy
to disappear the world.

Forgotten in the fog of well worn pathways,
habitual mindscapes: the delight at whales
breaching, at sea spume as it slants
toward waiting shore.

Sometimes it takes the screech
of blue jays, a psychedelic sunrise
to break the trance, to remember
the frailty and surprise of moth wings.

How startling the beauty of blooming
cardinal on a lip of lilikoi, succor
for a thirsty heart that needs
only to witness wonder.

How the freshness of presence,
aflame with possibility, is enough
to extinguish a thousand habits
like so much burnt wood.

No need to choose between tides
of the mind, the world's ebb and flow–
and silence. Weeping bamboo looks up
and smiles. No need to feel lonely.

A Hint of Peace

Imagine life
without complaint
no matter what arises.

Instead of *oh no,*
not this-not that
you can think, *this too-*

and this-

and this.

Living large
insists on room
for everything:

the honey and bitters
of sorrow, unhurried
joy, flowers among
paving stones, health
befriending illness,
the caw of crow
as an ambulance
passes, sirens raging.

If you can take what comes
without resistance:

snowflake or cannon shot,
the weight of lilies
in lightest breeze–

impossible fears, long
habits will crumble
and the heart will find its rest.

Dance Steps to the Edge of the Void

Desire is the Siren beckoning
just out of reach. A landscape, lush
or spare, horizon over the next hill
or beyond imagining. Slapstick
sunsets, cloud-sober skies. The howl
at moon shine or faintest flick of whisker;
you've caught the scent, you won't give
up that endless trail. Never self-limiting.
Never what you think it is.

Aversion: the trickster's mirror twin.
Avoiding plums too ripe for picking,
tarnished pennies, the peril of rain.
Loathing the disingenuous peddler,
the disowned impulse. Avoiding the
threat of loss to self, the suffering
of extremes. What is the difference
between wanting and not wanting?
What if the coin toss comes up empty?

Flow

Twilight gathers dusky wings
into long sleeves of evening,
dreams through the night.
Moon silk lights the way to dawn
awakening tide pools and travelers.

Wind moves between times with
ease as if knowing timelessness.
What if we could live as seamlessly
with no resistance? What if time
and matter didn't matter?

As sun pays homage to morning
in ribbons of mauve and apricot,
it leaves the rest of the day in our
hands. We can find grace beneath
small rocks or fault lines in sand.

In Search of the Changeless Heart

Death rides the hard crust of night.
Blued stars and cold spell moon
offer scant light, less comfort.

Everything we know about the body
lingers in the heart. But the heart
is not constant. It climbs on wings

of feather and bone to branches
honeyed like the arms of a lover,
drifts on fickle currents weaving

stories from habit and memory
laid over reality, then plunges
without warning into steep ravines

mired in the quicksand of emotion.
But death can free the heart to open
again; relinquishing belief in stories,

the yearning for solid ground, the heart
can fly free to whatever waits next
and rejoice in not knowing.

Dreaming Women in Rain
Ghazal for Agha Shahid Ali

On butterfly wings, Sophia rides the sea through early rain.
Her silken form skims an inky void in the dawning, in rain.

Indigo fans, jeweled clouds seed dreams of unseen realms.
How do we know she is not a mirage in the shimmering rain?

What of the widowed flower seller whispering underwater?
Who will tend the martyr's grave? Leave lilies in rain?

A neighbor is dressed in scarves of melancholy and amber.
With a crown of emeralds, she cries as she walks in the rain.

Nearby, an alabaster statue with gleaming sockets. Eyes
her lonely heaven and prays for Agha in the streaming rain.

In dream you could lose yourself in waves of snow and salt.
But then you would miss the exotic thrum, the flow of rain.

How do we feel joy in a world of concrete and sorrow?
The two year old boy knew wilted daisies longed for rain.

Forgiveness shapes the temple. Long shadows mourn.
We cover the bones of royal ancestors to protect their reign.

A thunderstorm sings to the neighbor's field in shades of granite.
Her lover unloved finds love again, takes refuge in wild rain.

Along a cobbled street, monks offer begging bowls to all beings.
Like Buddha, content to get nothing in return, they laugh at rain.

Softly

sift the soil as if it held the delicate shell
of your mother

an archaeology of dreams unfulfilled or pending:
astronaut adventurer marathon dancer

dig up her wishes layered as onion, replant
where memories of loss, disappointment

threaten to overrun days in cloud shadow
there is no way to know the flowers that bloomed

for a morning; their scent may have lingered
too faint for recognition

with life ephemeral as blaze of autumn leafing
fragile as moth wing in summer light

take no notice of strident voices or mud wasps
you know what this jewel is worth

what facets still face away from sun
it takes only the heart to turn them

Noticing

Watch how rain
drops
on an oil-slick,
black brim
of pavement,
how it washes
winter
from slovenly lanes
building altars
of twigs
and ticket stubs
to the unexpected.
How honeybees
hover,
sipping sweetly
from wet jasmine,
how taro leaves
make umbrellas
for storm-weary
toads.
What else
do we miss?

A Glimpse of Awakening

Spring drapes wet skirts over
greening earth. Secrets slip from
sensuous folds, seed the soil,
slow thoughts from churning.

Ideas will rise like waves, then
recede when left as they are. Like
breath, like tides and tornados,
like life, they have their rhythms.

Remaining undistracted as seasons
shift, swollen streams flood gardens
and barn swallows fly into dusty clouds–
wisdom blooms in small miracles.

Anahata, rare flower, opens
beyond thoughts of self or other
to embrace with loving kindness
the tiniest snail, the largest blunder.

Anahata: heart center

Infinity of Death

In this room of bones
and echoes,
of memory laid
down in amber
covering every surface
but mullioned window,
I look out and remember
sky will outlive me.

These walls of one day
crumbling adobe stand
blameless; they can't hold
back the dying that moves
like river through veins
of longing inscribed
in silk, I've woven,
then unraveled in my life.

It may be the single
thread that binds them,
diamond cutting through
thoughts and images
of self I've set in quicksilver-
the universal solvent leaving
only transparent, flickering
echoes-odes to the finite.

Changeless Awareness

Today: the death of yesterday,
tomorrow: the demise of today.
Will memories linger like cremation ashes,
empty particles held together by habit,
or will the heart let go into timeless love?

Each nanosecond dies to the next,
each moment, an offering of autumn
leaves rebirthing. What lasts?
What never changes? What can
you count on to always be there?

Not the fluid hours of summer
nor seasons of the mind, not
the weather of worldly attractions.
No trill of wood thrush or smile
of safflower lingers.

Amidst this ever-changing swirl of energy
and light, mosaic of motion and stillness,
an all-inclusive open heart, sweet
as mead, can taste the changeless–
touch the world.

Freedom

Take thimbles off your fingers
if you would be free. Dance
shoeless over still hot coals. Don't
bank your fires for the night.

Let your mind meander
unobstructed by clouds or sun.
Make no deliberate choices.
This or that, the same dream:

Life's thorns as welcome
as flowers. Leap like feather
on a gust of wind. Float unattached
down this river of mystery.

Let rain move you or bring you
to stillness. You have all the time
in all the universes. Not a moment
to spare. Dance-only dance.

Hozho

*Ekphrastic response to pot made my Max Early,
painted images by Norvin Johnson*

In night-dark vastness,
the timekeeper stands watch.
Your bones, moon-blanched,
marrow rich with ancestral stories,
form a *Hogan* of prophets and dreaming.
Guided by the north star's fire, your heart
wears a cloak of constellations circling:
Nahookkos Bi'ka', Nahookkos Bi'aad.
A channel of stars anoints your head.

Open to sky–*Ii'ni's* blessing,
the voice of thunder, calls lightning
then rain to consecrate your vessel,
beautify the land. My thirst is quenched,
spirit ignited. I can feel your heartbeat
beneath my feet. Serpent rising,
grandmother and grandfather dancing.

With feet of clay and hands toward
heaven, you walk in beauty.
Surrounded by the four holy mountains
in the four directions, the elements
in right relation, in oneness
with all that is around you,
in oneness with all that is within.
Above and below, everything sacred.
Hozho is restored.

Hogan: traditional Navajo home
Bi'ka', Nahookkos Bi'aad: Big Dipper; Cassiopeia
Ii'ni: thunderbird constellation
Hozho: harmony, beauty, natural order

Make Offerings

to those you venerate:
Buddha, Bodhisattvas, the ones
who dedicate their lives for us.
Jesus, Mary, Mother of mercy, all the saints
who help with everyday things.
Burn incense for the Unnamable Divine.
Offer prayers to deities, to mythic gods
and goddesses. To One or Many,
to the All. Remember the Ancestors.

When you're out in Nature, build a shrine
of stones and flowers. A single piece of fruit
will do. Feel the rain of blessings, then offer them
to city dwellers, to those who live in caves.

When you're eating, offer food to those have none
and pray that everyone can eat as well as you do.
Light a candle for those in darkness. Light the room
with gratitude for whatever you can think of.

Offer up everything: night terrors, the bliss of loving freely,
hopes and fears that make us human and bind us
to each other. Feed the hungry ghosts and demons.

When you're down or lonely, make offerings.
When you're waiting for your ride and traffic jams
will cause you to be late, make offerings.
Use your imagination.

Always give more than you receive. A smile, a large
gratuity for the waitress working two shifts in a row.
Kiss the postman for not opening your mail.

Worship generosity;
you cannot share too much.
If you give everything away,
you'll find that you have
more than you ever dreamed of.

When you are ill, pray that through your illness
others will not suffer. Offer them your healing
and exchange it for their misery or pain.

Breathe in the hardship, breathe in, transform
the violence of the world.
Breathe out your love and let it radiate
to fill all space.
Keep something in your pocket
for those who have less.
Help clear your elderly neighbor's yard.
Fertilize her lawn with kindness,
the key to *ahimsa*, no harm.

Make every moment an offering.
Supplicate for peace.
Sing the praises of garbage collectors

and window cleaners.
Prostrate to waterfalls and elephants.
Call on Tara, St. Theresa, pray for travelers
who help in war-torn places.

Each prayer of thankfulness, each petition
will set a butterfly free and warm the hand
of a political prisoner, giving small comfort.
Light butter lamps and bonfires.
Make offerings as if your life depended on it.

Section II
The Laughter of Stones

Blood of the Soil

I pour red wine onto sun-baked beds
of iris, rose and golden globe. Blue jade
vines swing from a pink tulip tree shading
the bronze Buddha that sits, peaceful,
on a platform of river rocks. The garden
is quiet but for leaves shimmying to the jazz
of morning breeze. My offering is silent,
grateful, opening to the elements' blessing,
to the vibrant love that is nature. Feeling
cloudless, I am planted deep as bitterroot,
the earth having swallowed my feet.
I breathe in the fragrance of grace,
the taste of enchantment, lean
toward the Buddha. He gives me a light.

Waking Up

Nature once again
has brought me
to my knees,
leveled my preferences
and must haves
with her unrelenting beauty.

Unrivaled, my thoughts
stand no chance
in the face of copper
sunsets, wide skyfuls
of passing clouds
and clear, open spaces.

I am a student of birdsong
seduced by honeysuckle,
flamboyant purple trumpets.
The wind spills wisdom
into my ears. I wake up
and listen.

Taos Summer

The dead fly on the windowsill
next to a magpie feather
reminds me to be humble.
On a bed shaped like Taos summer,
all rounded edges and sage,
I daydream in adobe. Cottonwoods
have abandoned me. Yesterday
they chattered through the night
but this morning wind moved
and left only the crows.
A spider drops from nowhere
and lands near my leg. I don't know
whether to run for the mountains
or enter her silent web. I allow her sticky,
silken strands to bind me to the physical
while singing bowls ring out
the sounds of emptiness. It's always
a question of balance. Do I leave
behind the poetry of my body,
its litany of suffering and bliss,
and journey to the Blue Lake
of my dreams? Or do I stay and dance
with spiders with only a glimpse
of filtered light through quaking
aspen? The dead fly speaks to me
of impermanence.

Traveling Light

I head up a narrow country
road to the highway, absorbed
in inner dialogue about some
perceived slight. Realize I am
lost in thought and ought to ask,
What more is there?, expand my
senses to include what's around:
pigs and sheep in a nearby
field, the small chocolate candy
shop, roosters crowing, a plane
overhead. I resolve to stay open.
Just then, a Tibetan monk
appears in this unlikely location
wearing red robes, head shaved
and covered by a baseball cap.
He walks past the car, ending
my one-sided conversation.
My earlier resentment
turns to awe.

The Door

A weathered plank door
watching over the studio speaks
to passersby in tones of chameleon.
If anyone looks vaguely official,
it squeaks like an unoiled hinge,
appears as disreputable as an old
storage locker or blends
into walls-voiceless, invisible.

For friend or angel, door sighs
like hollow reed, metal hasp at its heart
inviting a handshake, long body
stretching to soften its welcome.
For those who know reality,
the door is always open, revealing
the threshold between this world
and the next.

Descent

There were chestnuts in my soup
and my heart opened wide as the Nile
in summer. I was a pyramid longing,
yearning crop of corn and cabbages,
bored by the drama of ordinary things.

I excavated bones and planets,
bore children on an upturned
heron wing through tumult and roar
yet still I feared those soot-dark,
unexamined corners within.

Through tangles of twisted logic,
I followed uncertainty in doubtful colors.
Anxiety moldered beneath a thin veneer
of calm though I stopped short of looking
directly at my night terrors,

avoided that deepest well of unceasing
dread. An amber cloud of not knowing,
no control. Until I had no choice. Until
Persephone threw me into Hades'
realm and took my shoes.

I circled my own heart, drawn into
a vortex of apparitions, archetypes
and ebony snakes with searching

tongues-sinking in terror's quicksand.
Sinking into-myself.

Thoughts frozen in the seething
black were freed once owned,
foreboding eased as dawn's light
illuminated my mind. I heard
the laughter of surrender.

Stoned
Haibun for K

He was deaf to the wailing of river-tumbled rocks, the heartbeat of green things. His past had grown moss-rotting timbers in a once supple mind that threatened the calculus of his days. He lay under sky's pale wash: the tilt of sun and cloud chant softened his resistance to mourning dove's wisdom, calling him to open into being, to infinite, loving space–without thought or deadening habits to entrap him in familiar embrace, never let go. Tears of wisteria filtered the light, a prism of *what could be* floated just outside his vision waiting to take form. Suddenly, the world appeared in saturated hue and feeling, pure potential infused with joy.

No past to numb his present,
only the laughter of stream's
singing stones.

The Dalai Lama Speaks of Peace at the Maui War Memorial

I wished for a blessing
as I listened to the prayer
for all beings to have happiness
beyond hope and fear.

The day itself had proved a blessing,
gifts of compassion woven fine
as a monk's robe, nonviolence-
a rosary of good intentions

set against a balcony where army
snipers pointed rifles to secure
the peace loving audience
of followers and fans-a spiritual

Twilight Zone-yet no one wanted
to leave; his humility and joy
wrapped us in long yearned for
ease and openheartedness.

I was ready for a miracle.
Rainbows graced sun-blanched
skies outside the door, intensely hued
arches of perfection that mirrored

the perfection in construction sites

and roadways-nirvana in steel beams
and arching cranes. This display
of bliss and emptiness continued

as a peacock crossed the crowded
road in front of my car, all seeing
eyes of wisdom fanning out in full
feather, transforming my view.

Now You See It . . .

Sky has loved me
through every turning,
enfolded me in unclouded,
unconditioned space.
The coral vine
has christened me
with petals, a peach tree
has sung me out of dream.

Mango seeds large
as lemons soften my path
to the garden but soon
will sprout into myriad
trees unless uprooted
by pigs or pick axe.
Some loves are best
left unrequited.

I bow to the innocence
of willow. By honoring
the sacredness of slugs
and seedlings, perhaps I can
open to essence. These
landmarks may not be here
tomorrow. My habits
are coyotes laying false trails.

Always There

I squeeze all surprise from
the day, sift stones, read
mulberry leaves yet find
myself lacking in comfort.

There is nothing I can point to
in my usual mentation. I could
make up a story, blame it on
the stars or collective anxiety.

Although everything changes,
this angst often rides beneath
the surface like a deep sea diver
pointing down, away from light.

There are days I have covered
in roses, sat with their thorniness
and waited-until the ocean
calmed, waves subsided.

But not today. Today I will risk
everything. Turn the fear which
looms larger with nightfall into
curiosity. Befriend death.

A Simple Task

It was the blue-flowered dish
towel that made me think
of heaven and immortality,
had me drying dishes with
a tenderness of meaning.

How a thing so ordinary
can suddenly be numinous:
soap bubbles blessing a dish
before winking out or floating
off on transitory currents,

the purity of gleaming white plate,
the sparkle of stainless spoon.
I was carried on the breath
to a place of such tranquility,
there was no one drying

the dishes, only the astonishing,
all-consuming act of drying them.
Time left me then–and thought.
Dishes done, the world heart-
breakingly beautiful, I wept.

A Lover's Prayer

There is only one heart speaking
in tongues of earth and water—some
silver-soft and yearning, others
like smoke of serpents burning
in fires of unspent passion.

How can we know what lies in another's
heart? How can we sing in this realm
of the uncertain? When I think I am
clear, stars fall into my pocket, show
me I am still enclouded.

As long as I am lost in thought, I am
broken—projections flung carelessly into
a dying ocean. The space around me,
unruffled despite my frenzy, shimmers
with light awaiting recognition.

Even when the heart of the world
is breaking, there is always the frailty
of hope hinging on a lover's prayer,
the delicate sweetness of a life
beyond self that heals the future.

The Gift of Quietude

We climb a tree to keep you close,
write messages on bark
and seed pods with rabbit's feet.

Hidden beneath layers of fallen
leaves, ripening expectations
meet the power of death.

Like children on sand dunes,
our hearts comb the soil for treasure,
a kindness that is uncontrived.

Since there is compassion,
sun falls into the sea without thought.
Crows return to their nest.

An almost-song is carried on the breeze
by mating crickets; the mystery of moss
points the way north.

Since we are quiet, no one need learn
our secret: that we can open and fly
while oaks stay rooted for us.

Nothing to Do

You can blame it on the moon
or mustard seeds,
become a lotus in a pond
or borrow your sister's shoes.
You won't get there any faster,
won't get there at all
without letting go of what
you think you know, an offering
to fools and fantasists.

This is what I tell myself when
I'm pulled from ocean vastness
by waves of white noise roaring
about where I'm not and what's
not happening. My thoughts are
ashes covering sky, the glue
that holds a world in place, solid
as cobweb, for a universe
of one or many.

The feeling there is something
missing, something that I need
to do, is an empty ladder
to nowhere, suspended in space.
Letting the ladder go, free fall
with no support, there is nothing
to do but rest where I land,
wherever I am.

A Question of Love

What is the weight of water on sun-spackled hands?
What is the sound of cherishing?

I have wept for less than a penny's worth of grief,
laughed at moonstones harvested by thieves of night.

When is the sadness of a star-struck wanderer?
Will I open my arms to wind's siren call?

I asked my hands if they'd befriend each other.
Will my body ever leave its desert for home?

If suffering is a noble truth, what lies beyond death's habit?
The void seems such a busy place, open to everything.

Will my bones take heart when I feel love's longing?
Can I know the color of winter's kiss?

Where will my thoughts go when I give them the garden?
Will I remember to leave the gate always ajar?

Illusion's Beauty

Hugging the tree stump
like Hera's children,
they wear the green silk,
pink and lavender velvet
of Maypole ribbons.
Adorning earth's shoulders,
they bear early summer gifts.
I cannot walk by without
catching my breath.

When all else fails, when
world's shadow seems too
close, too real, there is always
beauty, always. I can find it
in the dark by touch, just
the other side of fear.
The fragrance of tuberose
on a bar of soap. The color
and texture of rust on cast iron.

Beauty knows no borders:
the bruised apple fallen
on the ground, lovely sight
to a deer, the transparent skin
shed by a garden snake,
the blue waterway
of an old woman's hands.

A discarded gun. Even
a bomb to the bomb maker.

My preference for flowers:
talisman for universal peace–
for earthworms and chameleons,
for kindness and the softness
of sea spray, is part of my dream–
insubstantial as a night rainbow
yet vivid. A beautiful illusion.

On Losing One's Head

Now the hawk finds shelter
from wind's bite and scissors.

Have you seen how it turns
its head around and tucks it
into back feathers for the night,
tender as a mother tending
her young? How it looks headless
perched with feet locked
on ulu limb?

How it can sleep through tempest
and thunder while I lie awake,
the slightest croak of frog, down-
pour or unwelcome thought
enough to keep dreams
at a distance?

Someone once told me, *So much
is possible when there is trust.*

Now the moon lends its eye
to a break in the storm. Hawk
sleeps on, no need for its head.
I envy its confidence.

Sparrow Encounter

I sat soft on sand
as swallows sang
and seagulls
rode swells
to search for
small fish.

A sparrow hopped
around the beach
as I succumbed
to sun. My thoughts
were dreamy,
indistinct.

I sighed and made
small chirping sounds
to greet the sparrow.
It approached, then
skittered back, came
closer as I stilled,

began to nibble at my
toes. Small forays back
and forth, it returned each
time to remain a bit longer.
And all I had to do–
stay open.

Weather Report

Last night, a gale
tossed mourning
clouds above the roof.
Rain pummeled tin,
wind pounded windows–
the turmoil of dreams
and demons, a topography
of transience.

One minute, storm
was a verb roaring through–
extravagant, unstoppable.
The next, a noun flat
as fallen leaf, ready to be
forgotten. Two doors down,
no rain at all, street dust-dry.
Weather report: arbitrary.

I waited for the next
dramatic outburst:
another downpour? hail?
my own unruly mental deluge?
Silence disconcerted me
until I found it at the core
of turbulence–
I gave up waiting.

Some Day

Some day I may know what a zebra dove sings
on the low hanging branch of *ohi'a* mid-morning,
what *'Io* carries on its flight through the valley.

The weight of understanding, weightless as contemplation
when grasping has fled, bends the wild orchid not at all,
settles within as the language of marigolds.

I've never seen geckoes hurry. When a cat stalks
a mongoose, there is no rush. No frantic worry it will miss
the prize. No thoughts of second chances.

When I'm patient as sky letting clouds pass, cardinals
come close and drink from a bowl near the fig tree.
If I think of myself, they quickly scatter and fly off.

Roses unfurl their sweet tea scent under sun's soft gaze.
Seeds drop and small rocks roll over in the garden
to make room; if only my mind knew this open secret.

ohi'a: Hawaiian flowering evergreen tree
'Io: Hawaiian hawk

No Need to Explain

I am falling in love with mystery-
all mystery-
from novel to numinous,
from knots of thought unraveling
leaving spaciousness, surprise
to the place of unknowing-
that limitless, open universe
beyond idea.

I wonder as I touch the petals
of an evening primrose
if it is also touching me, if I am
birthing passionfruit and petrels
as I embrace each morning.
I am delighted not to know
where thoughts go when
they've had their say,

where belief weighs heaviest
before it breaks like autumn
bough when I forget to hold on.
It is hard to be open when ego
seeks certainty like a homing pigeon,
distractions float as a mirage
before me and names like apple

tree and elephant stand in
for essence. What lies beyond
the veil of expectation?
A pebble drops into a pond,
a peacock calls. A neighbor
cries for a lost child.

Mapless

If I wait among
the blackberries
for rain to soften
thorns, lie down
among speckled
eggs readying
to hatch,
I will miss
the thrum of deeper
woods, wilding paths
with no promises.

Resisting the perfume
of convention,
the air
of authority,
I feel
compelled to follow
lines of desire,
pirate paths.
No maps needed,
only awareness.
Out of stillness,
signs will naturally
appear.

Inspiration

lay beneath a rock. Tall grass obscured it.
Rain singled out some blades over others,
clinging to the sides of unarticulated dreams.

Reaching down for something new,
I had to dig beneath habitual soil
full of the usual, the unrealized.

Nothing was obvious yet everything was there
needing only fresh water eyes, a sliver
of innocence to reveal the undiscovered.

A paradox to be unknotted: the search itself,
the obstacle. I made offerings to the muse, let
go of thoughts, settled. Releasing expectation,

I became a student of beginner's mind. I forgot
to be a poet, forgot my book but not my pen.
The rock lay bare, glistening.

Uncovered

Standing beneath an arch
of Buddha's belly bamboo,
I wait for the rain to stop,
for cabbage moths to resume
their flight, for Hawaiian crows
to leave their nests and forage.

I look for sun to reappear,
to feel its heat burn thought
away. I need to be naked here,
in this end of summer garden,
this place of memories
tumescent as spring rivers.

No need to forget, to live
as if thoughts are only
flowers on faded wallpaper.
No obstacle to being present
or enjoying this paradise
of pure awareness.

Stripped of all adornment,
I have only bare feet touching
earth, heart opened by
the unbridled rawness
of nature, sky's vast
unalterable space.

Without concepts, what do
I know? Only that I am here
watching the play of light
on ti leaves, the wind dance
of wrens and warblers.
I laugh at nothing.

Nesting

Dried leaves and twigs shaped round,
resting in the crook of a lemon tree.
A hint of blossoms to gentle night's air,
the intimacy of feathers settling in
to roost. A place for dreaming.

Safe . . . moon calls, igniting
the nest in lustrous nacre.
Remember you can wrap yourself
in solitude or claim the fellowship
of swallows and shadows.

Borrowing the wings of an owl, I search
my heart for the feeling of home, that
realm where my spirit can rest. Do I
need to let go of everything I know,
all that I am, to fly without reference
to a place I never left?

The Muse

has fastened her teeth to my leg
and hidden me from the moon. Her outer
shell-coarse, brown, ridged. Her other
side-smooth, blue pearl, lights me
in tiny sparks when I face away from sun.

Delicate as fern-like sea hair, unbending
as dead man's fingers, she has torn my heart
from its common moorings and insisted
I listen to the ocean. Really listen.
More than to tide and wave, to curl and froth.

Even gull songs are beside the point.
It takes slowing time, this kind of listening.
Deep in the marrow of place, the belly
of silence. Where I can feel seeds
germinate before there are names.

I am patient as a turtle sunning on lava.
For now, I relinquish the need to know.
Canaries chatter without my attending,
fish jump in tide pools, splashing unnoticed.
Exhilarated, I write to the incoming tide.

The Taste of Gratitude

When I remember
to thank a saffron finch
for serenades
at sunset, the dove
for morning matins,
the dahlia for sharing
its nectar with bees,
I am overcome
with love.
The air shimmers
as though seen
through flame,
a letting go
that frees
the senses,
slows the mind.
In that moment,
the world seems
to vibrate with joy
and my thoughts
are odes I sing
to the Divine.

Meditation Through the Night

The ancient stardust of my body
reclaims the night. Leaves me
trembling in the immensity.
There is nothing I can find outside.

Nothing I can say is mine.

Under moon's watchful brow, ocean
takes on the persona of a young girl
frolicking in lacy undergarments,
sapphire curls, seducing the shore.

Lover and beloved, where....

Coquis and cryptic cicadas pierce
the silence with their mating calls.
Yet nothing disturbs the calm. Not
even bamboo stalks clacking in storm.

When dawn arrives bringing color,
shadows lighten to palest ash.
Morning sounds glaze highways,
time to move into day.

Still, I remain in the timeless.

Section III
Geography of Stillness

At the Beginning

Settle your awareness
as gently as thistledown
on the rhythmic stream
of breath. Feel belly float
away from spine, return
like faithful friend-filling
with stardust, the dreams
of ancients, the wonder
of now. Then emptying
again and again, leaving
the world more radiant,
mind awake, at rest.

Grounding

feet sinking into
the earth
    settling
Buddha belly

feeling gravity's pull
    body resting
rooted like tree
weighted stone

nowhere to go
    nothing to do
mind everywhere
    yet undistracted

Space

The space between
thoughts
is not temporal
or spatial-
no clocks,
no past or future,

no substance
or lack of substance.

Awareness, always there
yet often not noticed,
taken for granted

until space opens up
like boundless sky
and thoughts and things
become background-

white noise.

Meditation on Watching Thoughts

Watching thoughts
can be a life sentence
for lovers of drama:
never ending stories
of the mostly irrelevant,
irreverent,
irritating,
boring and banal.
Occasionally insightful,
more rarely inspiring,
once in a great while
memorable.

Noticing without following,
without grasping
or expectations.
No need to embellish,
make more
or less
or anything other
than what appears–
is a day on the river
watching foreign films
with no subtitles.

When left as they are
without comment

or critique,
thoughts dissolve
like rainbows
in the space
of stillness.
Arise and fall away
unobstructed,
moving like mist
through mythic forest,
leaving reality in their wake.

A Geography of Stillness

Not the unmoving
silence of a gravestone.
Not only the gap
between thoughts
or the space between
thoughts and things
but a subtle, knowing calm
already present
that permeates everything.

At first my gaze finds
the between place,
thoughts slip south;
across the quiet expanse,
things move or not,
are silent or not.
Mind relaxes,
opens to the embrace
of pure awareness.

The Fullness of Emptiness

Since the world is within, I don't need
to seek love or feel unfulfilled. Yet desire
still rakes a path through morning leaves
for want of–
                something.

A simple walk wakes roots of yearning
yarrow; doves on a limb polish
riffs on unrequited courtship.
I feel–
                incomplete.

Surrounded by families of bowing ferns
and palm fronds, as thoughts drop away
like breeze-blown frangipani,
I find–
                peace.

Empty of concepts, the universe:
symphonic hologram, is full of
creative possibilities and wonder.
I am filled with–
                appreciation.

The seeds of stars leave their hulls behind,
burst forth, light years from awakening
or maybe only a moment away
when free of-
                          attachment.

Breathing into Stillness

When my thoughts are less
important than the wind, I hear
the sway of lemongrass,
cackling of bamboo, palm
sighs and pheasant calls, truck
gears grinding their way uphill.
The roar of silence in my ear–
a wave of sound that ebbs
with every burst of breeze.

I notice the dance of plumage
on coconut frond, a dash
of scarlet as a cardinal lands
on papaya leaf. All this
happens in the sacred space
that welcomes everything
to its field of movement
within stillness, a stillness
that permeates each breath.

Being

So where are the birds that would sing us
into pure dimensions, cloud free, light
sky with hints of liberation?

The mysterious domain of being. Guardians
at the gate of non-conceptuality: curiosity,
compassion, openness. And trust.

I have opened the door a sliver, maybe more;
new moon rises above dense clouds, tips
of the crescent peer bravely into space.

Big breath, belly aware of roots and flowers,
steadfast as mountain, steeped in earth's refrain.
The universe is kissed by radiance.

Looking within while eyes rest wide, I wonder if
I can float centerless, if I can let the fear that rises
arise without naming or becoming it.

Relaxing into nothing to do. What's different?
Nothing. Space for everything. No big deal.
Only ego gets lost. A case of mistaken identity.

New Year's Resolution

I'd like to give my   self
up for New Year's-
that necklace (or chain)
of thoughts and feelings
strung together with threads
of habit and memory
hanging heavy around my neck.

I might start by fasting
once a week-
abstaining from   self-ishness
sunrise to sundown-
not noticing how everything
affects me, putting others first-
not taking this   self
for real.

Perhaps I could try it
a day at a time like those
twelve step programs-
surrendering solidity and form
to openness, trading
the certainty of ego
for not knowing.

The Gift of Not Finding

What if   I
am just another habit,
convenient label
for a changing stream
ephemeral as mist?
What if I look and cannot
find this   I
and feel content
to rest just there?

Freedom?   Joy?   Liberation?

Letting Go

Siting near the Buddha in my garden
encircled by pink plumeria and fuchsia
peonies in full flower, it is easy to forget

what is missing. I resolve for today: I will not
want anything. The sounds of woodpeckers,
weedwackers, waterfalls will be more

than enough to fill me. Whatever arises, I will
think, *just so*. I will not even want to not want.
I will desire, need, grasp at-nothing.

What will endure? The smile of the Buddha,
that empty, lucid awareness full of everything.

Tapestry of Undivided Wholeness

Heal the deepest wound–
the ill(usion) of separateness–
and loneliness will fall away.
Like Mother Trees that network
with all other trees and flora,
we are jewels in this great web
of Indra, reflecting each other
infinitely, intimately intertwined.

Send compassion to dark states
so they will dissipate. Not even
discrete rock formations along
an eroding coastline are solid
or independent. The cry of gull
over ocean, the dance of dolphin
under Hecate's moon, evanescent
plays of luminance.

Seek kindness in the curl of leaf
a downpour brings, the laughter
of ptarmigans. Feel the love
in every breath we share
with lizards and lavender. Soften
the heart to open to the seen
and unseen, no distinction.
Take refuge in the blessing.

One Question

Mind squeezed by captivating thoughts
into narrow stream beds dried
by habitual rendering.

No apparent windows, the world
forgotten, dumpster in the alley
in shadow.

One question: *What else is there?*
frees mind to open, to include
a sublime array of colors, sounds,

shapes, sensations. Thoughts
rise and fall light as angora,
non-distracting.

Awareness-unmoved by the butterfly
that flits anywhere, alights
nowhere-abides like mountain.

Wisdom Blooms

Without the need to label
anything
mind's endless conversation
is a flower
and feelings rest on leaves
scattered by wind
to settle near hyacinths
and water lilies.

A bowl turned up in smile
holds the motion
of water
in an unruffled pond.
No need for misgivings
or even for dream.
Everything is
just as it is.

What Remains

Are you the space that appears as thought?

River stones?
Horizon's lip?
The sharp light of stars pointing to . . . ?

The awareness that recognizes space?

Without thought, will space prevail?
Will "I" disappear?

What remains
When ocean calms?
When rain settles on leafy boughs?

What if

we let expectations
        float   away
like so many squares of paper
on a storm-swept street?

No matter good or bad,
they constrict the   space
        around   them,
reduce awareness from   vast
to funnel.

How can we see what's always there
if we're blinded by labels?

How can we recognize something so close
yet subtle? so precious yet easy?

What are we waiting for?

Not the Way You Think

Not there or not-there,
solid or insubstantial,
separate or inseparable.
Without differentiating
self and not-self,
inside and out.
Beyond judgments
of good and bad,
right and wrong.
Free of all concepts-
a whole universe awaits:
a silky, joyful isness,
a delicious suchness
where wisdom whispers
from every gorgeous
flower and corner,
in every quivering,
shining moment,
where clarity
blazes forth
like diamonds
in a snow field,
piercing mind's
illusions, bringing
infinite gratitude
for life.

Prayer flags

When I exhale,
the Tibetan flags
suspended from a shelf
above my desk flutter
sending prayers
into the world.

Now when breezes
move through leaves
of the golden shower
tree and neighboring
coconut palms, I see
them as prayer.

When wind ripples
river, it sets small
stones afloat, carries
twigs and koa branches
toward the ocean
as offerings.

Is movement arising
out of stillness
prayer?
And is stillness
the sacred ground?

The Turn

That longed for presence and peace:
always already here. Apparent
in the way that moon sends tendrils
of light through reverent branches
and opens the beaks of nightingales
to sing their devotions. It doesn't
require silence or an absence
of thought. In the midst of chaos,
fury of cyclone or cacophony of conflict-
just beneath those turbulent waves
and eddies, lies a vast ocean of calm
fed by streams of kindness. Unnoticed,
its underlying love seems unmanifest.
Yet even the slightest turn of the mind
in any moment reveals it.

As Earth's Rotation Slows

So as to
ensure the world still turns
despite a backwards drag,
kiss the sunlight that promises
morning and offer yourself
to each grain of sand.

So as to
affirm the earth does not shift poles
when life slips into a deep abyss,
listen to roses when they speak
in scents of incomplete sentences.
Rely on your luminous essence.

So as to
know this life as transient dream,
trust what your senses don't perceive,
the changeless at the heart of change.
Become the mirror reflecting a world,
awareness without the dreamer

Ode to the Emptiness of Moon

A camera cannot capture
moon's fragile beauty, how
it silvers leaf tips and shimmers
a path from horizon to shore.
Words can only point to
sunflowers lifting their heads,
wiliwili trees their branches
in honor of its fullness.

Ineffable, we delight at moon's
appearance in sky's night.
Unknowable, we sense its cool
glistening. Its moonness
remains just out of reach,
an idea with no substance.
Wondrous, how it lingers
momentarily in the expanse.

Unnamed

Mystical silence
of pomegranate seeds,
serenity-sensual spores
of every possibility
floating in and out
of awareness,
red-clovered feet running
through meadow's hush
unaltered by sound

Silence so rich
it flames with radiance.
Background to foreground,
phenomena arise
and dance with wonder,
ornament awareness,
fade back into stillness.
The heart's magic,
mind's nature.

Essential Nature

Not the thoughts
or feelings
that arise
and pass away
like so many
dust motes
floating past
the window.

The sounds
of barking
neighbor dog
and flutter
of dragonfly:

A symphony.

Not the things
mind perceives
out there or within:
a river flowing
by, the movie
inside, the growl
of an empty
stomach.

But the awareness
that projects,
perceives
and knows
all this –
always there.

Nothing else.

The Gift Of (   )

What can I share: a bowl of apples in an empty
room, the fragrance of lilacs through a broken
window. A parrot feather in a basket of dreams.
A marathon of thoughts leading (   ).

What can I give: my breath made of starlight,
the marrow of ancients, neighboring
flowers, devotion of mourning doves.
The gift of equanimity in the midst of (   ).

When I give up the illusion of a self and all
stories drop away, all separation, I can offer
the everything of everything, hold nothing back,
drifting on the joyful wind of recognition.

Who knows

what pears eat?
How blackbirds sway
to music
only they can hear?
What knows
this moment,
this life
of charred hopes,
quince blossoms
ready to fruit?
What is this knowing
that knows it is knowing-
unchanged, unconditioned
by the awareness of knowing?

Let Be

The I
holds
closed
a door
the eye
cannot
see.

Beyond,
beneath,
behind,
before...
the bliss
of all
possibility.

No key
needed,
no flight
to get
an eagle's
view.

Right here
in the heart,
in that
vast,
uncontrived
space,

knots
loosen,
borders
fall away
and the door
         opens
              on its own,
                       into
                             the
                                     boundless.

Dancing in the Heart of the Void

At the edge of endings:
contraction, a staccato
hush. The fluted flower
draws bees to their last
supper. A scattering
of entrails, jagged cut,
the lamentation of ravens.

Beginnings: before the
final leaf falls, the loss
of meaning-a seed
ruptures, shoots green
beneath hard fundament,
awaits softening, the breath
of dragonflies.

Coming or going, ever-shifting
forms appear like clouds, play
on the ground of awareness
before dissolving. No dancer
at the beginning, no dancer
at the end. Only the joy
of the dance.

About the Author

Carol Alena Aronoff, Ph.D. is a psychologist, teacher and writer who co-founded SAGE, a psycho-spiritual program for elders; helped guide a Tibetan Buddhist Meditation center for seven years; taught Eastern spirituality and practices, imagery, meditation, and women's health at San Francisco State University for nearly fourteen years. She guided Healing in Nature retreats in Hawaii and the Southwest, and had a counseling practice in Marin County for many years. She co-authored *Practical Buddhism: The Kagyu Path* with Ole Nydahl in 1989 and edited five books and four meditation booklets on Tibetan Buddhism. Dr. Aronoff published a textbook: *Compassionate Healing: Eastern Perspectives* in 1992.

Her poetry has been published in *Comstock Review, Potpourri, Poetic Realm, Poetica, Mindprints, Dream Fantasy International, Beginnings, Hawaii Island Journal, In Our Own Words, Theater of the Mind, Animals in Poetry, From the Web, HeartLodge, Out of Line, Sendero, Buckle&, Iodine, Asphodel, Tiger's Eye, Nomad's Choir, Cyclamens & Swords, Tale Spinners, Poet's Lane, The New Verse News, Expressing Bridges, Quill & Parchment, Nature Writing.com, Lilipoh, Avocet., Bosque, Zingara, Pyrokinection, Jellyfish Whispers, The Ghazal Page, Origami, Sourland Review, Vox Poetica, Panoplyzine, Amethyst Review, Young Ravens Literary Review, The Beautiful Space- A Journal of Mind, Art and Poetry, Minute Magazine, Otherwise Engaged Journal, Total Eclipse, Verse of Silence, Foreign Literary Journal* and *The Wild Word*. Her poems have also appeared in numerous anthologies: *Out of Line, 200 New Mexico Poems,*

Women Write Resistance, Before There is Nowhere to Stand, Malala: Poems for Malala Yousafzai, The Four Seasons, Poetry of the American Southwest, Secrets/Dreams, Tranquility, Dove Tales: Empathy in Art: Embracing the Other, Shattered, Elementary My Dear, Jeté Away, Without Words, and *You Can Hear the Ocean: An Anthology of Classic and Current Poetry.*

She received a prize in the 1999/2000 Common Ground spiritual poetry contest, judged by Jane Hirshfield, and was twice a Pushcart Prize nominee. She won the *Tiger's Eye* contest on the writing life and has participated a number of times in *Braided Lives*, a collaboration of artists and poets as well as in SKEA's *Art and Nature* event, *Ekphrasis: Sacred Stories of the Southwest*, and *(A) Muses Poster Retrospective* for the 2014 Taos Fall Arts Festival. She was judge for the 2008 *Tiger's Eye* poetry contest.

A chapbook of Native American/Hawaiian poems, *Cornsilk*, was published by Indian Heritage Council in 2004, and her illustrated poetry book, *The Nature of Music*, was published by Pelican Pond/Blue Dolphin Publishing in 2005. An expanded, illustrated *Cornsilk* was published in 2006, *Her Soup Made the Moon Weep*, in 2007 and *Blessings from an Unseen World* in 2013. *Dreaming Earth's Body: poems by Carol Alena Aronoff, paintings by Betsie Miller-Kusz* was published in 2015. The poetry collection, *Tapestry of Secrets*, was published by Finishing Line Press in 2019. Currently, Carol Aronoff resides in a rural area of Hawaii--working her land, meditating in nature and writing.

www.ingramcontent.com/pod-product-compliance
Lightning Source LLC
Chambersburg PA
CBHW030337100526
44592CB00010B/723